Design and typography by Alec Viana

Mind Prints by
Frank Meo

Dear Sara,

all the best!

Frank

2010

www.capturedinthemind.com

The book is dedicated to Sylvia, Emilia and Nicky. They help me each day to imagine.

Thanks to Jeff Grossman, Mark Rosen, Judy and Brian McLaughlin, Jim and Susan Hornecker, Cazzie Russell, Justin Rosen, Dr. Barry Gordon, Andy and MaryAnn Geller, Ivan Geldzahler, Allan Luftig, Willie Mays, Brian and Anya Tomko, Michael Ginsberg, Susan and Steve Thomas, Wendy Umanoff, BJ Kocen, Shelley Friars, Linda and Fred Hahn, Sheldon Crooks, Vincent Meo, John Serruto, Won S. Im, Paul Cappelli, Renee Bavineau, Casey Kelbaugh, Baldev Duggal, John Timen, Demian Cacciolo, Rosa Santiago, Jessie Paterson and Louisa Curtis.

Frank Meo | Captured in the Mind

What's on your mind? How do you think? In words or in images?

We all collect images we've seen in the course of our days. But there's even more: how about all the images we created ourselves, in our minds, images of things we haven't actually seen, and of which no photos exist, things that the paparazzi missed; images that we created based on media accounts, water cooler discussions.
What if somebody curated these images, strung them up in a gallery show for you to walk through and see, clearly and consciously..?

This is what Frank Meo is hoping to do with this project: help you discover the creativity of your own mind!
Frank Meo's background is in advertising. He has his own company, MeoRepresents, representing commercial photographers and photojournalists. So he knows very well about the power of images.

Meo has collaborated with designer, Alec Vianu to design this book with a simplicity and directness that treats the concept and the viewer with dignity and respect.

He also knows about people. He's a Brooklyn boy, born into an Italian working class family, growing up mostly in the ball parks, which shaped his very keen sense of street smarts, his 20/20 vision So when he feels like he's taken for a ride, he usually doesn't need to wait for as explanation. He reacts – quickly and strongly.
This is what triggered this project.

The idea for Mind Prints was born while visiting the Guggenheim Museum's Richard Prince show in 2007. In some of his most famous works, as member of the early image world generation, Prince used photos from the Marlboro Ads - cropped, without the lettering - and framed them as fine art pieces for us to focus on their more complex social ramifications. But there is no reference to the commercial photographer who originally took the photo -offensive especially for anybody working in advertising. To Meo, there also seemed to be an underlying sense of arrogance - the well educated, insightful artist, putting his finger on the shortcomings of the common man: this dream of the heroic cowboy, the bikers' girlfriends on the back covers of magazines, the fascination with attractive nurses.

Frank Meo doesn't judge. People are his lifeline. He always finds a way to relate. And more than that, he also always finds ways of bringing people together, which is what he did in the making of this project.
The project has grown as people added their own favorite mind prints to the collection. Each hanging invites discussions, additions. People feel empowered and inspired. It is truly socially interactive. And here's the major difference that sets Frank Meo's work apart from most conceptual art works: it remains close to the people, it is a project that resonates with everybody, even if they are not immersed in the art world.

The images that Meo's Mind Prints evoke are those of intriguing, iconic moments of our times. The fact that most of us actually think of these moments in images, not only words, proves how much our minds have been shaped by over a century of photographs inundating our world. Robert Rauschenberg, Andy Warhol, the Pop artists and Richard Prince

introduced the media photos as part of our visual environment that became the source of their art. By now, we've started to take it for granted that photos and cameras are omnipresent. Mostly everything is documented in pictures. Facebook has made photographing (not just looking at photographs) an intrinsic part of our children's search for identity. Indispensable. At times it seems like we can only look consciously, if it is through a camera.
So how come there is no photo of Lacy being dumped into the lake, Clinton with Monica Lewinsky? What do we do when there's no photo at hand? Has our upbringing in the image world trained our imagination enough, so that we can create the missing images in our mind? Has the media crafted our art of working around the black hole, so that we can easily fill the gap? Doesn't the media sometimes even try to find images that match our expectations or popular imagination, rather than trying to capture the unexpected, estranging truth.

Frank Meo says 'yes' — we all create these images in our minds — they're our works, intriguing, ingenious and very worth being brought to life by his Mind Prints!

Sylvia Laudien
New York, 2009

Artists have long had an intuitive grasp of how to break through the doors of perception and seize the minds hiding behind those doors.

Frank Meo's MindPrints extends that tradition. He presents us with words on the printed page, adds typographic design, and with the combination evokes images unseen yet strangely familiar. They tickle, bemuse, perhaps even repulse. But they all make us feel these experiences, as though we had glimpsed them ourselves.

Why Frank's MindPrints can make this happen in our heads is now better understood by cognitive science and cognitive neuroscience. The marks on the page are abstract patterns of letters that our brain transparently converts into thoughts (and sounds). The initial thoughts may go no further, or they may provoke others. Some of these thoughts and connections have been lying latent in our brains and minds, imprinted by our experience, but dormant. Some will be brand-new, only brought into existence by the words on the page. But unlike ordinary words in ordinary type, the words, the typography, and the arrangements on the page in MindPrints have been carefully chosen to resonate, reinforce, amplify and extend the images and emotions that the words qua words have evoked. Some of the pages will FLASH! --- detonate circuits in our brain, explosively setting off chains of associations. Others will build up more slowly, gradually gaining force as they meander through our minds and recruit other thoughts and experiences. Ultimately, the synaptic activity sparked by these MindPrints will die down, electrically and chemically. But they will leave traces -- some stronger, some weaker -- of latent connections, priming us for future experiences.

It is very likely that we will not even consciously recall the original experience, the original MindPrint, that changed the way we think and react. But all of them will transform our brains.

Enjoy MindPrints as an artistic experience. But also appreciate that MindPrints are probes into the way your own mind works, Rorschach tests of modern experiences. This understanding of the neural science behind MindPrints should do nothing to diminish your enjoyment. If anything, it should double your appreciation of both Mr. Meo's artistry and the boundless qualities of our minds.

Barry Gordon, M.D., Ph.D.
Therapeutic Cognitive Neuroscience Professor
Professor of Neurology and Cognitive Science
The Johns Hopkins Medical Institutions
Baltimore, MD

Your first time
_____

Warhol and Mappletrop

in a bathtub.

Al Gore

creating
the
internet.

Monica

(with a Cigar)

When Obama knew

Titanic

Sinking

Weapons of Mass Destruction

Yogi Berra at

the fork in the Road

Lorraine Bobbitt

Osama bin Laden

in a cave.

Planes coming in 92nd floor, WTC

OJ fighting with
Ron Goldman

Reagan says "Nyet"

OJ fighting with
Ron Goldman

Reagan says "Nyet"

to Gorbachev

(click)

Zapruder with his camera

Michael Vick at

a dog fight.

Barbaro being put down

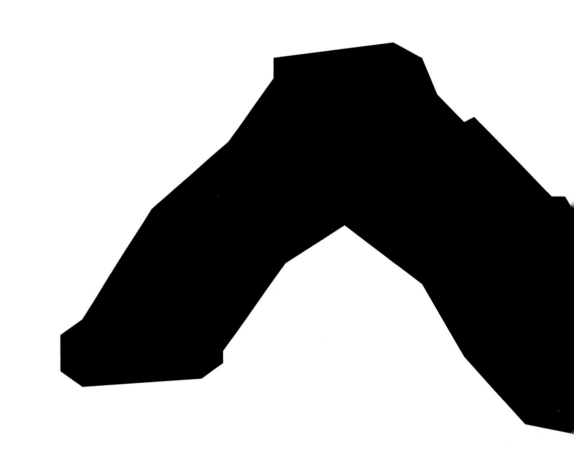

Romans approaching Masada

Atta in the cockpit

Gore and Lieberman
the night they gave up

Joe Namath Superbowl
guarantee

J. Edgar Hoover in a dress

Jimmy Hoffa at
Giants stadium

Back of
Monica's
head.

CLEMENS TAK

ING STEROIDS

Dylan in the Chelsea Hotel

Pete Rose with
his bookie

Scott Peterson dumping Lacey's
body

Tower of Pisa -
straight

Richard Gere with Gerbil

Liberace

in his underwear

Van Gogh

with a knife

Lady Di in the car

Ted Bundy
with

a coed

DEEP THROAT with Woodward and Bernstein

Jeffery Dahmar eating a meal

John Lennon at
the Dakota

Bonds applying
"the clear"

Ron Jeremy losing
his mojo

Hitler in bunker

Ted Kennedy

on the Chappaquiddick

bridge

Steve Irwin being pierced by a Stingray.

Trump
(with morning hair)

JonBenet Ramsey in
the closet

Keith Richards
writing
"Satisfaction"

When Bill t

old Hillary

Nixon and Kissinger drunk

Menendez parents on couch

"We go to war"

Osama bin Laden in Hell

UNABOMBER,

Theodore Kaczynski, in
the post office

Mama Cass Elliot
with a ham sandwich

Atta in cockpit

Martha Stewart doodling in prison

Bernie Goetz on
the subway

Curtis Sliwa in
a cab with John Gotti jr.

Marv Albert in
women's underwear

Howard Cosell without toupe

Sonny Bonno hitting a tree

BEATLES with

their LAWYERS

Anita Hill,

Clarence Thomas with a can of coke

****

***** Michael Jackson with little boys. ***

don imus &

rutgers girls

"

——— ——————————

———————————

————————————

————————. "

Harpo speaks.